INTRODUCTION TO CYBERSECURITY

Protecting Your Digital World: A Beginner's Guide

BY

ROBERT WILLIAMS

Table of contents

Chapter 1: Introduction to Cybersecurity

In today's interconnected digital world, cybersecurity has become a critical concern for individuals, businesses, and governments alike. This chapter serves as an introduction to the fundamental concepts of cybersecurity, highlighting its importance, tracing its evolution, and elucidating why it's relevant to everyone.

Understanding the Importance of Cybersecurity:
Cybersecurity encompasses the protection of digital systems, networks, and data from malicious attacks and unauthorized access. With the proliferation of internet-connected devices and the exponential growth of digital data, the potential impact of cyber threats has escalated dramatically. From personal identity

theft to large-scale data breaches affecting millions of individuals, the consequences of cybersecurity breaches can be severe and far-reaching.

The interconnected nature of modern society means that virtually every aspect of our lives relies on digital technology, from communication and commerce to healthcare and transportation. As such, the security of our digital infrastructure is essential to safeguarding our privacy, financial well-being, and even physical safety.

Brief History and Evolution of Cyber Threats:
The history of cybersecurity traces back to the early days of computing when the primary concern was protecting mainframe systems from unauthorized access. As technology advanced and the internet became ubiquitous, new forms of cyber threats emerged, ranging from computer viruses and worms to sophisticated hacking techniques.

Over the years, cyber attacks have grown in frequency, sophistication, and impact. Notable incidents, such as the Morris Worm of 1988, the ILOVEYOU virus of 2000, and the WannaCry ransomware attack of 2017, have demonstrated the devastating consequences of cyber vulnerabilities and the need for robust cybersecurity measures.

As technology continues to evolve, so too do cyber threats. The rise of interconnected devices in the Internet of Things (IoT), the increasing reliance on cloud computing, and the proliferation of artificial intelligence present new challenges and opportunities for cyber attackers.

Why Everyone Needs to Be Concerned about Cybersecurity:
In the digital age, cybersecurity is no longer solely the concern of IT professionals and security experts. Every individual who uses

digital devices or accesses the internet is potentially vulnerable to cyber threats. Whether it's protecting personal information from identity theft, safeguarding financial accounts from fraud, or ensuring the integrity of communication channels, cybersecurity touches virtually every aspect of our daily lives.

Moreover, the interconnected nature of digital systems means that a security breach affecting one entity can have cascading effects across entire networks and industries. For businesses, the financial and reputational damage resulting from a cybersecurity incident can be catastrophic, leading to loss of customer trust, regulatory penalties, and even legal liabilities.

In summary, cybersecurity is a fundamental aspect of modern life that affects individuals, businesses, and society as a whole. By understanding the importance of cybersecurity, recognizing the evolving nature of cyber threats, and embracing proactive measures to mitigate risks, we can collectively build a safer and more resilient digital ecosystem.

Chapter 2:
Fundamentals of Cyber Threats

In this chapter, we delve into the fundamentals of cyber threats, exploring the various types of threats, common attack vectors, and real-world examples to illustrate the ever-present dangers lurking in the digital landscape.

Types of Cyber Threats:

Cyber threats come in many forms, each with its own unique characteristics and objectives. Malware, short for malicious software, is one of the most pervasive and damaging types of cyber threats. It includes viruses, worms, Trojans, ransomware, spyware, and adware, among others. Malware is designed to infiltrate systems, disrupt operations, steal sensitive information, or extort money from victims.

Phishing is another prevalent cyber threat that relies on social engineering techniques to deceive users into divulging personal information, such as login credentials or financial details. Phishing attacks often take the form of fraudulent emails, text messages, or websites masquerading as legitimate entities.

Other common cyber threats include denial-of-service (DoS) and distributed denial-of-service (DDoS) attacks, which aim to overwhelm a target system or network with an excessive volume of traffic, rendering it inaccessible to legitimate users. Additionally, insider threats, supply chain attacks, and zero-day exploits pose significant risks to organizations and individuals alike.

Common Attack Vectors and Techniques:

Cyber attackers employ a variety of tactics and techniques to exploit vulnerabilities and compromise systems. These attack vectors can target network infrastructure, software applications, hardware components, and human vulnerabilities.

Some of the most common attack vectors include:

- **Exploiting software vulnerabilities**: Attackers exploit weaknesses in software applications or operating systems to gain unauthorized access or execute malicious code.

- **Social engineering**: Attackers manipulate human psychology to trick users into divulging sensitive information or performing actions that compromise security.

- **Brute force attacks**: Attackers attempt to gain unauthorized access to systems by systematically guessing usernames and passwords until they find the correct combination.

- **Man-in-the-middle attacks**: Attackers intercept communication between two parties to eavesdrop on sensitive information or manipulate data exchanges.

- **SQL injection**: Attackers inject malicious SQL code into web applications to extract or manipulate data stored in databases.

Real-World Examples of Cyber Attacks:
Examining real-world examples of cyber attacks helps to illustrate the severity and diversity of cyber threats. From high-profile data breaches at multinational corporations to targeted attacks against critical infrastructure, the impact of cyber attacks can be profound and wide-ranging.

For instance, the Equifax data breach of 2017 exposed the personal information of over 147 million individuals, including names, social security numbers, and credit card details, highlighting the vulnerability of centralized databases to cyber exploitation.

Similarly, the Stuxnet worm, discovered in 2010, was a sophisticated cyber weapon designed to sabotage Iran's nuclear program by targeting industrial control systems. This unprecedented cyber attack demonstrated the potential for cyber warfare to disrupt critical infrastructure and geopolitical stability.

In summary, understanding the fundamentals of cyber threats is essential for navigating the complex and ever-evolving landscape of cybersecurity. By recognizing the various types of threats, common attack vectors, and real-world examples, individuals and organizations can better prepare themselves to defend against cyber attacks and mitigate potential risks.

Frequently Asked Questions And Answers

1. What are the most common types of cyber threats?

   - The most common types of cyber threats include malware (viruses, worms, Trojans, ransomware), phishing attacks, denial-of-service (DoS) attacks, social engineering scams, and insider threats.

2. How do cyber attackers gain access to systems and networks?

   - Cyber attackers use various attack vectors to gain unauthorized access to systems and networks, including exploiting software vulnerabilities, social engineering techniques, brute force attacks, and phishing emails.

3. What are some signs that my computer or network has been compromised by malware?

- Signs of a malware infection may include unusual system behavior (e.g., slow performance, frequent crashes), unauthorized changes to files or settings, unusual network activity, and unexpected pop-up messages or advertisements.

4. How can I protect myself against phishing scams?

- To protect yourself against phishing scams, it's essential to be cautious of unsolicited emails, avoid clicking on suspicious links or attachments, verify the authenticity of websites before entering sensitive information, and enable spam filters and email validation tools.

5. What steps can I take to secure my home network?

- To secure your home network, you can start by changing the default passwords on your router and Wi-Fi network, enabling encryption (WPA2 or WPA3) for wireless connections, disabling remote management features, and keeping router firmware up to date.

6. Are there any real-world examples of cyber attacks that I should be aware of?
   - Yes, there have been numerous high-profile cyber attacks in recent years, including data breaches at major corporations (e.g., Equifax, Yahoo), ransomware attacks targeting hospitals and government agencies, and state-sponsored cyber espionage campaigns (e.g., Stuxnet, NotPetya).

7. What should I do if I suspect that my computer or network has been compromised?
   - If you suspect that your computer or network has been compromised, it's essential to take immediate action to minimize the damage. This may include disconnecting from the internet, running antivirus scans to detect and remove malware, changing passwords for compromised accounts, and notifying relevant authorities or IT support personnel.

Chapter 3: Protecting Your Digital Identity

In this chapter, we explore strategies and best practices for safeguarding your digital identity in an increasingly connected and data-driven world. From managing passwords to encrypting sensitive information, protecting your digital identity is paramount to ensuring your privacy and security online.

Password Security Best Practices:

Passwords serve as the first line of defense against unauthorized access to your accounts and sensitive information. However, many people still use weak, easily guessable passwords or reuse the same password across multiple accounts, putting themselves at risk of account compromise.

To enhance password security, it's essential to follow best practices such as:

- **Use strong, complex passwords:** Create passwords that are at least 12 characters long and include a mix of uppercase and lowercase letters, numbers, and special characters.

- **Avoid using easily guessable information:** Refrain from using common words, phrases, or personal information (such as birthdays or pet names) in your passwords.

- **Enable multi-factor authentication (MFA):** Whenever possible, enable MFA to add an extra layer of security to your accounts. This typically involves providing a second form of verification, such as a code sent to your phone or a biometric scan.

- **Use a password manager:** Consider using a reputable password manager to generate and store complex passwords securely. Password managers can also help you keep track of your credentials across multiple accounts.

Two-Factor Authentication (2FA) and Multi-Factor Authentication (MFA):

Two-factor authentication (2FA) and multi-factor authentication (MFA) are additional security measures that require users to provide two or more forms of verification to access their accounts. In addition to entering a password, users may need to provide a one-time code sent to their phone or email, use a biometric scan, or insert a physical security key.

By enabling 2FA or MFA, users can significantly enhance the security of their accounts and reduce the risk of unauthorized access, even if their passwords are compromised.

Secure Data Storage and Encryption:

Encrypting sensitive information is essential for protecting it from unauthorized access, both in transit and at rest. Encryption converts data into an unreadable format that can only be deciphered with the appropriate decryption key, making it virtually impossible for unauthorized individuals to intercept or decipher the information.

When storing sensitive data, such as financial records, personal documents, or confidential communications, it's crucial to use encryption to prevent unauthorized access or data breaches. Many modern operating systems and applications offer built-in encryption features, and there are also third-party encryption tools available for additional security.

Protecting your digital identity requires a combination of strong password practices, multi-factor authentication, and encryption. By implementing these security measures, you can mitigate the risk of unauthorized access to your accounts and sensitive information, safeguarding your privacy and security in an increasingly digital world.

Frequently Asked Questions And Answers

1. What are the best practices for creating strong passwords?

- Strong passwords are at least 12 characters long and include a mix of uppercase and lowercase letters, numbers, and special characters. Avoid using easily guessable information such as birthdays or pet names, and refrain from using the same password across multiple accounts.

2. How does multi-factor authentication (MFA) enhance security?

- Multi-factor authentication requires users to provide two or more forms of verification to access their accounts. This adds an extra layer of security beyond just a password, making it more difficult for attackers to gain unauthorized access.

3. What are the benefits of using a password manager?

- Password managers generate and store complex passwords securely, eliminating the need to remember multiple passwords for different accounts. They also offer features such as auto-fill and automatic password generation, streamlining the login process while enhancing security.

4. Why is encryption important for protecting sensitive data?

- Encryption converts data into an unreadable format that can only be deciphered with the appropriate decryption key. By encrypting sensitive information, you can prevent unauthorized access or interception, ensuring the confidentiality and integrity of your data.

5. How can I ensure the security of my personal documents and files?

- To secure personal documents and files, you can use encryption tools to encrypt sensitive data before storing it on your devices or transferring it over the internet. Many operating systems and applications offer built-in encryption features for added security.

6. Is it safe to store sensitive information in the cloud?

   - Cloud storage services offer convenience and accessibility, but it's essential to take precautions to secure sensitive information stored in the cloud. This includes using strong, unique passwords, enabling multi-factor authentication, and encrypting data before uploading it to the cloud.

7. What should I do if I suspect that my digital identity has been compromised?

   - If you suspect that your digital identity has been compromised, take immediate action to secure your accounts and mitigate potential damage. This may include changing passwords, enabling multi-factor authentication, monitoring account activity for suspicious behavior, and notifying relevant authorities or IT support personnel.

Chapter 4: Securing Your Devices and Networks

In this chapter, we delve into the essential aspects of securing your devices and networks against cyber threats. With the proliferation of internet-connected devices and the increasing complexity of network infrastructures, protecting your digital assets from malicious actors is more critical than ever.

Understanding Firewalls and Antivirus Software:
Firewalls and antivirus software are two foundational components of cybersecurity that help protect your devices and networks from unauthorized access and malicious software.

- Firewalls: A firewall is a network security device that monitors and controls incoming and outgoing network traffic based on predetermined security rules. Firewalls act as a barrier between trusted internal networks and untrusted external networks, filtering traffic to prevent unauthorized access and block potentially harmful data packets.

- Antivirus Software: Antivirus software, also known as anti-malware software, is designed to detect, prevent, and remove malicious software from your devices. Antivirus programs scan files, emails, and web traffic for known malware signatures and behavioral patterns, quarantining or deleting threats to prevent them from compromising your system.

It's essential to keep your firewall and antivirus software up to date to ensure they can effectively defend against the latest cyber threats.

Updates and Patch Management:

Software vulnerabilities are a common target for cyber attackers seeking to exploit weaknesses and gain unauthorized access to systems. To mitigate this risk, software vendors regularly release updates and patches to fix known vulnerabilities and improve security.

It's crucial to prioritize and apply software updates and patches promptly to ensure your devices and applications remain protected against the latest threats. Many operating systems and software applications offer automatic update features that can streamline the patch management process and reduce the risk of exploitation.

Safe Browsing Habits and Avoiding Malicious Websites:

Web browsing is a common vector for cyber attacks, with malicious actors often using phishing websites, fake download links, and malicious advertisements to trick users into downloading malware or revealing sensitive information.

To mitigate the risk of encountering malicious websites, it's essential to practice safe browsing habits, such as:

- Only visiting trusted websites with secure HTTPS connections
- Being cautious of unsolicited emails, links, and attachments
- Verifying the authenticity of websites before entering sensitive information
- Using ad blockers and browser extensions that offer additional security features

By adopting safe browsing habits and avoiding malicious websites, you can reduce the likelihood of falling victim to cyber attacks while browsing the internet.

Securing your devices and networks requires a multi-faceted approach that includes implementing firewalls and antivirus software, keeping software up to date with regular updates and patches, and practicing safe browsing habits. By taking proactive measures to protect your digital assets, you can mitigate the risk of cyber threats and safeguard your privacy and security online.

Frequently Asked Questions And Answers

1. What is a firewall, and how does it protect my devices and network?

   - A firewall is a network security device that monitors and controls incoming and outgoing traffic based on predetermined security rules. It acts as a barrier between trusted internal networks and untrusted external networks, filtering traffic to prevent unauthorized access and block potentially harmful data packets.

2. Why do I need antivirus software, and how does it work?

   - Antivirus software is essential for detecting, preventing, and removing malware from your devices. It works by scanning files, emails, and web traffic for known malware signatures and behavioral patterns, quarantining or deleting threats to prevent them from compromising your system.

3. How can I ensure that my software and operating systems are up to date?

- To ensure that your software and operating systems are up to date, enable automatic updates whenever possible. Many operating systems and software applications offer automatic update features that can streamline the patch management process and reduce the risk of exploitation.

4. What are some safe browsing habits to avoid malicious websites and downloads?

- To avoid malicious websites and downloads, be cautious of unsolicited emails, avoid clicking on suspicious links or attachments, verify the authenticity of websites before entering sensitive information, and use ad blockers and browser extensions that offer additional security features.

5. How can I secure my home network from cyber threats?

- To secure your home network, change the default passwords on your router and Wi-Fi network, enable encryption (WPA2 or WPA3) for wireless connections, disable remote management features, and keep router firmware up to date with regular updates and patches.

6. What should I do if I suspect that my device or network has been compromised?

- If you suspect that your device or network has been compromised, take immediate action to minimize the damage. This may include disconnecting from the internet, running antivirus scans to detect and remove malware, changing passwords for compromised accounts, and notifying relevant authorities or IT support personnel.

Chapter 5: Social Engineering and Phishing Awareness

In this comprehensive chapter, we delve into the deceptive world of social engineering and phishing scams, shedding light on the tactics used by cybercriminals to manipulate individuals and organizations into divulging sensitive information or performing actions that compromise security.

Understanding Social Engineering:

Social engineering is a psychological manipulation technique used by cyber attackers to trick individuals into divulging confidential information, performing actions, or bypassing security controls. Unlike traditional hacking methods that rely on technical exploits, social engineering exploits human vulnerabilities, such as trust, curiosity, and fear, to achieve its objectives.

Common social engineering techniques include pretexting (creating a false pretext or scenario to elicit information), baiting (enticing victims with something desirable to extract information or compromise security), and tailgating (physically following someone into a restricted area to gain unauthorized access).

Recognizing Phishing Emails and Messages:

Phishing is a prevalent form of social engineering that involves sending fraudulent emails, text messages, or other electronic communications masquerading as legitimate entities to deceive recipients into revealing sensitive information, such as usernames, passwords, or financial details.

To recognize phishing emails and messages, it's essential to look out for common red flags, such as:

- Urgent or threatening language designed to evoke fear or panic.
- Requests for sensitive information, such as login credentials or financial details.
- Suspicious links or attachments that may lead to malicious websites or malware downloads.
- Poor grammar, spelling errors, or inconsistencies in the email content.

By being vigilant and cautious when interacting with unsolicited emails or messages, individuals can reduce the risk of falling victim to phishing scams and protect their personal and financial information from unauthorized access.

Strategies for Avoiding Social Engineering Attacks:

Preventing social engineering attacks requires a combination of awareness, education, and proactive measures. Some strategies for avoiding social engineering attacks include:

- **Employee training and awareness programs**: Educating employees about the various types of social engineering attacks, common tactics used by cybercriminals, and best practices for identifying and reporting suspicious activity can help empower them to recognize and thwart potential threats.

- **Implementing security policies and procedures:** Establishing clear security policies and procedures for handling sensitive information, verifying the identity of individuals requesting access or information, and conducting regular security audits can help mitigate the risk of social engineering attacks.

- **Using technical controls and safeguards:** Implementing technical controls such as email filtering and anti-phishing tools, multi-factor authentication, and access controls can help prevent unauthorized access and limit the impact of social engineering attacks.

By adopting a multi-layered approach to security that combines employee training, security policies, and technical controls, organizations can strengthen their defenses against social engineering attacks and reduce the likelihood of successful compromises.

Social engineering and phishing scams pose significant threats to individuals and organizations alike, exploiting human vulnerabilities to gain unauthorized access to sensitive information or systems. By understanding the tactics used by cybercriminals, recognizing common red flags, and implementing proactive security measures, individuals and organizations can better protect themselves against social engineering attacks and mitigate potential risks.

Frequently Asked Questions And Answers

1. What is social engineering, and how does it differ from traditional hacking methods?

   - Social engineering is a psychological manipulation technique used by cyber attackers to trick individuals into divulging sensitive information or performing actions that compromise security. Unlike traditional hacking methods that rely on technical exploits, social engineering exploits human vulnerabilities, such as trust and curiosity, to achieve its objectives.

2. How can I recognize phishing emails and messages?

   - Phishing emails and messages often contain common red flags, such as urgent threatening language, requests for sensitive information, suspicious links or attachments, and poor grammar or spelling errors. By being vigilant and cautious when interacting with unsolicited emails or messages, individuals can reduce the risk of falling victim to phishing scams.

3. What should I do if I receive a suspicious email or message?

- If you receive a suspicious email or message, it's essential to refrain from clicking on any links or attachments, avoid providing sensitive information, and report the suspicious activity to your organization's IT security team or email provider. Most email providers offer tools for reporting phishing emails to help protect other users from similar attacks.

4. How can I protect myself and my organization from social engineering attacks?

- Protecting against social engineering attacks requires a combination of awareness, education, and proactive measures. This includes implementing security policies and procedures, conducting employee training and awareness programs, using technical controls such as email filtering and multi-factor authentication, and staying informed about the latest social engineering tactics and trends.

5. What are some common social engineering tactics used by cybercriminals?

- Common social engineering tactics include pretexting (creating a false pretext or scenario to elicit information), baiting (enticing victims with something desirable to extract information or compromise security), phishing (sending fraudulent emails or messages), and tailgating (physically following someone into a restricted area to gain unauthorized access).

6. How can I educate employees and raise awareness about social engineering attacks?

- Educating employees about social engineering attacks and raising awareness about common tactics and red flags is essential for preventing successful compromises. This can be achieved through employee training programs, simulated phishing exercises, and regular communication about emerging threats and best practices for staying safe online.

Chapter 6: Safe Online Behavior

In this comprehensive chapter, we explore the importance of safe online behavior and provide practical guidance for individuals to protect themselves and their personal information while navigating the digital landscape. From safeguarding personal information to managing privacy settings on social media platforms, adopting safe online behavior is essential for maintaining privacy, security, and peace of mind in an interconnected world.

Protecting Personal Information Online:
One of the first steps in practicing safe online behavior is to protect personal information from falling into the wrong hands. This includes being cautious about sharing sensitive information such as full names, addresses, phone numbers, and financial details on public forums, social media platforms, and other

online channels. It's important to be mindful of who you share information with and to only provide personal details to trusted sources.

Privacy Settings on Social Media Platforms:

Social media platforms play a significant role in our online interactions, but they also present privacy risks if not managed carefully. To protect your privacy on social media, it's essential to review and adjust your privacy settings regularly. This includes controlling who can see your posts, photos, and personal information, limiting the audience for your content, and being selective about accepting friend requests or connections from unknown individuals.

Securing Online Accounts and Credentials:

Securing online accounts and credentials is crucial for preventing unauthorized access to sensitive information and digital assets. This includes using strong, unique passwords for each account, enabling multi-factor authentication whenever possible, and monitoring account activity for suspicious behavior. It's also essential to be cautious of phishing scams and to avoid clicking on suspicious links or downloading attachments from unknown sources.

Understanding the Risks of Public Wi-Fi:

Public Wi-Fi networks are convenient for staying connected on the go, but they also pose security risks if not used securely. When using public Wi-Fi, it's important to avoid accessing sensitive information or logging into accounts that contain personal or financial data. Instead, consider using a virtual private network (VPN) to encrypt your internet connection and protect your privacy while using public Wi-Fi networks.

Safe Online Shopping and Financial Transactions:

Online shopping and financial transactions are convenient but can also be risky if proper precautions are not taken. To shop safely online, only make purchases from reputable websites with secure payment methods, such as HTTPS encryption and payment processors like PayPal or credit cards. Avoid entering sensitive financial information on unsecured websites or responding to unsolicited emails requesting personal or financial details.

Protecting Children and Families Online:

For families with children, ensuring their safety and privacy online is paramount. This includes setting age-appropriate limits and guidelines for internet use, monitoring children's online activities, and educating them about the importance of safe online behavior. It's also essential to use parental control tools and privacy settings to restrict access to inappropriate content and protect children from online threats.

Practicing safe online behavior is essential for protecting personal information, maintaining privacy, and safeguarding against online threats. By being vigilant, proactive, and informed about potential risks and best practices, individuals and families can navigate the digital world with confidence and peace of mind.

Frequently Asked Questions And Answers

1. How can I protect my personal information online?

   - To protect your personal information online, it's essential to be cautious about sharing sensitive information on public forums, social media platforms, and other online channels. Only provide personal details to trusted sources, use strong, unique passwords for each account, and enable multi-factor authentication whenever possible to prevent unauthorized access.

2. What are some best practices for managing privacy settings on social media platforms?

   - Review and adjust your privacy settings regularly on social media platforms to control who can see your posts, photos, and personal information. Be selective about accepting friend requests or connections from unknown individuals, and consider limiting the audience for your content to trusted friends and family members.

3. How can I secure my online accounts and credentials?

- Secure your online accounts and credentials by using strong, unique passwords for each account, enabling multi-factor authentication whenever possible, and monitoring account activity for suspicious behavior. Be cautious of phishing scams and avoid clicking on suspicious links or downloading attachments from unknown sources.

4. Is it safe to use public Wi-Fi networks?

- Public Wi-Fi networks can be convenient for staying connected on the go, but they also pose security risks if not used securely. Avoid accessing sensitive information or logging into accounts that contain personal or financial data when using public Wi-Fi. Consider using a virtual private network (VPN) to encrypt your internet connection and protect your privacy while using public Wi-Fi networks.

5. What are some tips for safe online shopping and financial transactions?

- When shopping online or conducting financial transactions, only make purchases from reputable websites with secure payment methods, such as HTTPS encryption and payment processors like PayPal or credit cards. Avoid entering sensitive financial information on unsecured websites or responding to unsolicited emails requesting personal or financial details.

6. How can I protect my children and family members online?

- Protecting children and family members online involves setting age-appropriate limits and guidelines for internet use, monitoring online activities, and educating them about safe online behavior. Use parental control tools and privacy settings to restrict access to inappropriate content and protect children from online threats.

Chapter 7: Secure Communication and Data Transfer

In this comprehensive chapter, we explore the importance of secure communication and data transfer in protecting sensitive information from interception or unauthorized access. From understanding encryption basics to using secure messaging platforms and virtual private networks (VPNs), ensuring the confidentiality and integrity of communication channels is essential for maintaining privacy and security in the digital age.

Encryption Basics:
Encryption is a foundational technology for securing communication and data transfer by converting plaintext information into ciphertext, which can only be deciphered with the appropriate decryption key. There are two

primary types of encryption: symmetric encryption, where the same key is used for both encryption and decryption, and asymmetric encryption, where separate public and private keys are used.

Symmetric encryption is faster and more efficient but requires a secure method for sharing encryption keys between parties. Asymmetric encryption, on the other hand, provides greater security by using a public key for encryption and a private key for decryption, eliminating the need to exchange keys securely.

Secure Messaging and Email Services:
Secure messaging and email services play a crucial role in protecting the confidentiality and integrity of communication channels. These services often use end-to-end encryption to ensure that messages are encrypted on the sender's device and decrypted only on the recipient's device, preventing interception or eavesdropping by third parties.

Popular secure messaging platforms, such as Signal, WhatsApp, and Telegram, offer features like end-to-end encryption, self-destructing messages, and verification mechanisms to authenticate users and protect against impersonation or tampering.

Virtual Private Networks (VPNs) for Enhanced Privacy:

Virtual private networks (VPNs) are another essential tool for securing communication and data transfer, especially when accessing the internet over untrusted networks, such as public Wi-Fi hotspots. A VPN creates a secure, encrypted connection between the user's device and a remote server, hiding the user's IP address and encrypting data to prevent interception by third parties.

VPNs offer several benefits, including:

- Masking the user's IP address and location to enhance privacy and anonymity.

- Encrypting internet traffic to protect against eavesdropping and surveillance.

- Bypassing geographic restrictions and censorship by accessing content from different regions.

When choosing a VPN service, it's essential to select a reputable provider with robust encryption protocols, a strict no-logs policy, and a clear commitment to user privacy and security.

Emerging Trends and Future Challenges:

As technology continues to evolve, new trends and challenges are emerging in the realm of secure communication and data transfer. These include the widespread adoption of encrypted messaging apps, the integration of encryption into mainstream communication platforms, and the increasing importance of privacy-preserving technologies, such as zero-knowledge proofs and homomorphic encryption.

However, alongside these positive developments, there are also emerging challenges, such as the proliferation of surveillance technologies, government efforts to weaken encryption for law enforcement purposes, and the potential misuse of encryption by malicious actors for illicit activities.

Secure communication and data transfer are essential for protecting sensitive information and maintaining privacy and security in an increasingly interconnected world. By understanding encryption basics, using secure messaging and email services, leveraging virtual private networks (VPNs), and staying informed about emerging trends and challenges, individuals and organizations can enhance the confidentiality and integrity of their communication channels and safeguard

their digital assets against unauthorized access
and interception.

Frequently Asked Questions And Answers

1. What is encryption, and why is it important for secure communication?

- Encryption is a technology that converts plaintext information into ciphertext, which can only be deciphered with the appropriate decryption key. It is essential for secure communication because it ensures that sensitive information remains confidential and protected from unauthorized access or interception by third parties.

2. How do secure messaging and email services protect user privacy and security?

- Secure messaging and email services employ end-to-end encryption to ensure that messages are encrypted on the sender's device and decrypted only on the recipient's device. This prevents interception or eavesdropping by third parties and ensures the confidentiality and integrity of communication channels.

3. What are virtual private networks (VPNs), and how do they enhance privacy and security?

- Virtual private networks (VPNs) create a secure, encrypted connection between the user's device and a remote server, hiding the user's IP address and encrypting data to prevent interception by third parties. VPNs enhance privacy and security by masking the user's online activities and protecting against eavesdropping and surveillance.

4. Are all VPN services equally secure and trustworthy?

- Not all VPN services are equally secure and trustworthy. When choosing a VPN service, it's essential to select a reputable provider with robust encryption protocols, a strict no-logs policy, and a clear commitment to user privacy and security. Additionally, users should be cautious of free VPN services, as they may compromise user privacy by logging or selling user data.

5. What are some emerging trends and challenges in secure communication and data transfer?

   - Emerging trends in secure communication include the widespread adoption of encrypted messaging apps, the integration of encryption into mainstream communication platforms, and the increasing importance of privacy-preserving technologies such as zero-knowledge proofs and homomorphic encryption. However, there are also challenges, such as government efforts to weaken encryption for law enforcement purposes and the potential misuse of encryption by malicious actors for illicit activities.

6. How can individuals and organizations ensure the confidentiality and integrity of their communication channels?

   - To ensure the confidentiality and integrity of communication channels, individuals and organizations can adopt encryption technologies, use secure messaging and email services with end-to-end encryption, leverage virtual private networks (VPNs) for enhanced privacy and security, and stay informed about emerging trends and best practices in secure communication.

Chapter 8: Cybersecurity for Businesses

In this comprehensive chapter, we delve into the world of cybersecurity for businesses, exploring the challenges, strategies, and best practices for protecting organizational assets, data, and operations from cyber threats. From risk management to incident response planning, cybersecurity is essential for businesses of all sizes to safeguard against financial losses, reputational damage, and legal liabilities.

Understanding Cybersecurity Risks for Businesses:

Businesses face a myriad of cybersecurity risks, including data breaches, ransomware attacks, insider threats, and supply chain vulnerabilities. These risks can result in financial losses, disruption of operations, loss of customer trust, and regulatory penalties. Understanding the potential impact of cyber threats is the first step in developing an effective cybersecurity strategy for businesses.

Risk Management and Cybersecurity Governance:

Effective risk management is essential for identifying, assessing, and mitigating cybersecurity risks within an organization. This involves establishing cybersecurity governance structures, policies, and procedures to ensure that security controls are implemented, monitored, and continuously improved over time. Key components of risk management include risk assessment, risk mitigation planning, and regular risk monitoring and review.

Employee Training and Awareness Programs:

Employees play a critical role in maintaining cybersecurity within an organization, but they can also be a source of risk if not properly trained and educated about cybersecurity best practices. Implementing employee training and awareness programs can help raise awareness about common cyber threats, teach employees how to recognize and respond to potential risks, and promote a culture of cybersecurity awareness and vigilance.

Implementing Technical Controls and Safeguards:

Technical controls and safeguards are essential for protecting organizational assets and data from cyber threats. This includes implementing firewalls, intrusion detection systems, endpoint security solutions, and encryption technologies to prevent unauthorized access, detect suspicious activity, and encrypt sensitive information. Regular security assessments and penetration testing can help identify vulnerabilities and weaknesses in an organization's systems and infrastructure.

Developing an Incident Response Plan:
Despite best efforts to prevent cyber attacks, organizations must also be prepared to respond effectively in the event of a security incident. Developing an incident response plan outlines the steps to be taken in the event of a data breach, ransomware attack, or other cybersecurity incident, including incident detection, containment, eradication, recovery, and post-incident analysis. Regular testing and rehearsal of the incident response plan are essential to ensure readiness and effectiveness in a real-world scenario.

Compliance and Regulatory Considerations:
Compliance with cybersecurity regulations and industry standards is essential for businesses to protect sensitive data, maintain customer trust, and avoid legal liabilities. Depending on the

industry and geographic location, businesses may be subject to various cybersecurity regulations, such as the General Data Protection Regulation (GDPR), the Health Insurance Portability and Accountability Act (HIPAA), or the Payment Card Industry Data Security Standard (PCI DSS). Ensuring compliance with these regulations requires ongoing monitoring, assessment, and implementation of security controls and measures.

In summary, cybersecurity is a critical concern for businesses in today's digital age, requiring proactive measures, investment, and commitment to protect organizational assets, data, and operations from cyber threats. By understanding cybersecurity risks, implementing effective risk management practices, providing employee training and awareness, implementing technical controls and safeguards, developing an incident response plan, and ensuring compliance with regulatory requirements, businesses can enhance their cybersecurity posture and mitigate potential risks and impacts of cyber attacks.

Frequently Asked Questions And Answers

1. What are the most common cybersecurity risks for businesses?
   - Businesses face various cybersecurity risks, including data breaches, ransomware attacks, insider threats, phishing scams, and supply chain vulnerabilities. These risks can lead to financial losses, operational disruptions, reputational damage, and legal liabilities.

2. How can businesses effectively manage cybersecurity risks?
   - Effective risk management involves identifying, assessing, and mitigating cybersecurity risks through comprehensive risk assessments, implementation of security controls, and continuous monitoring. Establishing a cybersecurity governance framework, with clear policies and procedures, ensures that risk management efforts are coordinated and aligned with business objectives.

3. Why is employee training important for cybersecurity, and what should it include?

- Employees are often the first line of defense against cyber threats but can also be a weak link if not properly trained. Employee training should cover topics such as recognizing phishing emails, using strong passwords, understanding social engineering tactics, and following data protection protocols. Regular training and awareness programs help create a culture of cybersecurity within the organization.

4. What technical controls and safeguards should businesses implement to protect their assets?
- Businesses should implement a range of technical controls and safeguards, including firewalls, intrusion detection and prevention systems, endpoint security solutions, encryption technologies, multi-factor authentication, and regular software updates. Conducting regular security assessments and penetration testing helps identify and address vulnerabilities.

5. What is an incident response plan, and why is it important for businesses?
- An incident response plan outlines the steps an organization should take in the event of a cybersecurity incident, such as a data breach or

ransomware attack. It is crucial for minimizing damage, ensuring a swift recovery, and maintaining business continuity. The plan should include procedures for incident detection, containment, eradication, recovery, and post-incident analysis. Regular testing and rehearsal of the plan ensure its effectiveness.

6. How can businesses ensure compliance with cybersecurity regulations and standards?

- Compliance with cybersecurity regulations and standards, such as GDPR, HIPAA, and PCI DSS, requires ongoing monitoring, assessment, and implementation of security controls. Businesses should stay informed about relevant regulations, conduct regular compliance audits, and document their security measures and practices. Engaging with legal and compliance experts can help ensure adherence to regulatory requirements.

7. What should businesses do if they experience a data breach or cyber attack?

- If a business experiences a data breach or cyber attack, it should immediately activate its incident response plan. Key steps include containing the breach to prevent further damage, eradicating the threat, recovering affected systems and data, notifying affected parties and regulatory authorities if required, and conducting a post-incident analysis to identify lessons learned and improve future security measures.

8. How can small businesses with limited resources enhance their cybersecurity?

- Small businesses can enhance their cybersecurity by focusing on key areas such as employee training, using strong passwords and multi-factor authentication, implementing basic technical controls like firewalls and antivirus software, regularly updating software and systems, and backing up critical data. Partnering with managed security service providers (MSSPs) can also provide access to advanced security tools and expertise.

Chapter 9: Cloud Security

In this comprehensive chapter, we explore the critical aspects of cloud security, which has become increasingly important as more organizations migrate their data, applications, and infrastructure to cloud environments. Cloud security encompasses the policies, technologies, and controls designed to protect data, applications, and the associated infrastructure in the cloud from threats and vulnerabilities.

Understanding Cloud Security Fundamentals:
Cloud security involves a shared responsibility model between the cloud service provider (CSP) and the customer. This model delineates the security responsibilities of each party. The CSP is typically responsible for securing the underlying cloud infrastructure, including physical data centers, hardware, and core services. The customer, on the other hand, is responsible for securing their data, applications, and configurations within the cloud environment.

Key areas of focus in cloud security include:

1. **Data Security:** Ensuring that data stored in the cloud is protected against unauthorized access, breaches, and loss.
2. **Identity and Access Management (IAM):** Controlling who has access to cloud resources and what actions they can perform.
3. **Network Security:** Protecting cloud networks and communications from attacks and intrusions.
4. **Compliance and Legal Issues:** Adhering to regulatory requirements and standards relevant to cloud environments.

Data Security in the Cloud:
Data security is paramount in cloud environments, as sensitive information is often stored and processed in the cloud. Key practices for securing data in the cloud include:

- **Encryption:** Encrypting data both at rest and in transit to prevent unauthorized access. This involves using strong encryption protocols and managing encryption keys securely.
- **Data Loss Prevention (DLP):** Implementing DLP solutions to detect and

prevent data breaches, leaks, and unauthorized data transfers.

- **Backup and Recovery:** Regularly backing up data and having robust recovery plans in place to restore data in case of loss or corruption.

Identity and Access Management (IAM):

IAM is crucial for controlling access to cloud resources and ensuring that only authorized users can perform specific actions. Key IAM practices include:

- **Multi-Factor Authentication (MFA):** Requiring multiple forms of verification before granting access to cloud resources.
- **Role-Based Access Control (RBAC):** Assigning permissions based on roles to limit access to necessary resources only.
- **Least Privilege Principle:** Granting users the minimum level of access required to perform their job functions, reducing the risk of accidental or malicious actions.

Network Security in Cloud Environments:

Securing cloud networks involves protecting data as it travels between users, devices, and cloud services. Key practices for network security include:

- **Virtual Private Networks (VPNs):** Using VPNs to create secure, encrypted connections for accessing cloud resources.
- **Firewalls and Security Groups:** Implementing firewalls and configuring security groups to control inbound and outbound traffic to cloud resources.
- **Intrusion Detection and Prevention Systems (IDPS):** Deploying IDPS to monitor network traffic for suspicious activity and respond to potential threats.

Compliance and Legal Issues:
Organizations using cloud services must comply with various regulatory requirements and standards, depending on their industry and geographic location. Key considerations include:

- **Data Residency and Sovereignty:** Ensuring that data is stored and processed in compliance with local laws and regulations, which may have specific requirements regarding data residency and sovereignty.
- **Regulatory Compliance:** Adhering to industry-specific regulations such as GDPR for

data protection, HIPAA for healthcare, and PCI DSS for payment card security.

- **Auditing and Reporting:** Maintaining detailed logs and reports to demonstrate compliance with regulatory requirements and support audits.

Emerging Trends and Challenges in Cloud Security:

As cloud adoption continues to grow, new trends and challenges are emerging in the realm of cloud security. These include:

- **Hybrid and Multi-Cloud Environments:** Managing security across hybrid (on-premises and cloud) and multi-cloud environments presents unique challenges, requiring comprehensive strategies and tools to ensure consistent security policies and controls.

- **Serverless and Container Security:** As organizations adopt serverless computing and containerization, securing these technologies involves addressing new attack vectors and vulnerabilities specific to these environments.

- **Artificial Intelligence (AI) and Machine Learning (ML):** Leveraging AI and ML for cloud security can enhance threat detection, response, and overall security posture. However, it also introduces new risks and challenges, such as securing AI/ML models and preventing adversarial attacks.

Frequently Asked Questions And Answers

1. What is the shared responsibility model in cloud security?

- The shared responsibility model in cloud security delineates the security responsibilities between the cloud service provider (CSP) and the customer. The CSP is responsible for securing the underlying cloud infrastructure, including physical data centers, hardware, and core services. The customer is responsible for securing their data, applications, and configurations within the cloud environment.

2. How can businesses ensure data security in the cloud?

- Businesses can ensure data security in the cloud by implementing strong encryption for data at rest and in transit, using data loss prevention (DLP) solutions, regularly backing up data, and having robust recovery plans in place to restore data in case of loss or corruption.

3. What are best practices for Identity and Access Management (IAM) in the cloud?

- Best practices for IAM in the cloud include using multi-factor authentication (MFA) to enhance security, implementing role-based access control (RBAC) to limit access based on roles, and following the principle of least privilege to grant users the minimum level of access required to perform their job functions.

4. How can organizations secure their cloud networks?

- Organizations can secure their cloud networks by using virtual private networks (VPNs) to create secure, encrypted connections, implementing firewalls and security groups to control traffic, and deploying intrusion detection and prevention systems (IDPS) to monitor network traffic for suspicious activity and respond to potential threats.

5. What are the key compliance and legal considerations for cloud security?

- Key compliance and legal considerations for cloud security include ensuring data residency and sovereignty in compliance with local laws, adhering to industry-specific regulations such as GDPR, HIPAA, and PCI DSS, and maintaining detailed logs and reports to demonstrate compliance and support audits.

6. What challenges do hybrid and multi-cloud environments present for security?

- Hybrid and multi-cloud environments present challenges such as managing security across diverse platforms, ensuring consistent security policies and controls, and addressing potential vulnerabilities and attack vectors specific to each environment. Comprehensive strategies and tools are required to effectively manage and secure these complex environments.

7. How can organizations secure serverless and containerized environments in the cloud?

- Securing serverless and containerized environments involves implementing best practices such as securing the code and configuration of serverless functions and containers, monitoring for vulnerabilities, using container orchestration tools securely, and ensuring that security policies are applied consistently across all instances.

8. How can artificial intelligence (AI) and machine learning (ML) be used for cloud security?

- AI and ML can enhance cloud security by improving threat detection, automating response to incidents, and analyzing vast amounts of data to identify patterns and anomalies. However, securing AI/ML models and preventing adversarial attacks are critical challenges that must be addressed to leverage these technologies effectively.

9. What steps should organizations take to respond to a security incident in the cloud?

- In the event of a security incident, organizations should activate their incident response plan, which includes steps for incident detection, containment, eradication, recovery, and post-incident analysis. It's essential to regularly test and update the incident response plan to ensure its effectiveness.

10. What factors should be considered when choosing a cloud service provider (CSP) for security?

- When choosing a CSP, organizations should consider factors such as the provider's security protocols and certifications, compliance with relevant regulations, the availability of security features and tools, the shared responsibility model, and the provider's track record and reputation for security.

Chapter 10:
Cybersecurity in the
Internet of Things (IoT)

We explore the critical aspects of cybersecurity within the rapidly growing field of the Internet of Things (IoT). IoT refers to the network of physical devices—ranging from home appliances to industrial machinery—that are connected to the internet, enabling them to collect and exchange data. While IoT offers significant benefits in terms of efficiency, convenience, and innovation, it also introduces unique cybersecurity challenges due to the vast number of connected devices and their often limited security features.

Understanding the IoT Landscape:
The IoT landscape is diverse and expansive, encompassing various sectors such as healthcare, manufacturing, transportation, agriculture, and smart cities. IoT devices include everyday consumer products like smart thermostats and fitness trackers, as well as critical infrastructure components like industrial control systems and medical devices. The connectivity and data exchange capabilities

of these devices open up new opportunities for cyber attacks, making robust security measures essential.

Key IoT Security Challenges:
Several factors contribute to the unique security challenges in the IoT ecosystem:

1. **Device Diversity and Scale:** The sheer number and variety of IoT devices, each with different hardware, software, and communication protocols, create a complex security landscape.
2. **Resource Constraints:** Many IoT devices have limited processing power, memory, and energy resources, which can restrict the implementation of robust security measures.
3. **Long Lifespan and Lack of Updates:** IoT devices often have long lifespans and may not receive regular software updates or patches, leaving them vulnerable to new threats.
4. **Network Complexity:** IoT devices can connect to various networks, including home, corporate, and public networks, increasing the attack surface and potential entry points for cyber threats.

Fundamental Principles of IoT Security:

To address these challenges, IoT security must be built on fundamental principles that guide the development, deployment, and management of IoT devices and systems. These principles include:

1. **Secure by Design:** Security should be integrated into the design and development process of IoT devices, ensuring that devices have built-in security features and are resilient to attacks from the outset.

2. **Authentication and Authorization:** Implementing strong authentication and authorization mechanisms ensures that only legitimate users and devices can access IoT networks and data.

3. **Data Encryption:** Encrypting data both at rest and in transit protects sensitive information from unauthorized access and interception.

4. **Regular Updates and Patch Management:** Ensuring that IoT devices receive regular software updates and security patches helps protect them from known vulnerabilities and emerging threats.

5. **Network Segmentation:** Segregating IoT devices into separate network segments can limit the spread of an attack and protect critical systems from being compromised.

Implementing IoT Security Measures:
Effective IoT security requires a combination of technical, organizational, and procedural measures. Key security measures include:

1. **Device Authentication and Access Control:**
   - Use strong, unique credentials for each device to prevent unauthorized access.
   - Implement multi-factor authentication (MFA) for accessing IoT systems and management interfaces.
   - Employ role-based access control (RBAC) to limit access to IoT data and functionality based on user roles and responsibilities.

2. **Secure Communication Protocols:**
   - Use secure communication protocols, such as Transport Layer Security (TLS), to encrypt data transmitted between devices and the cloud or other network endpoints.
   - Avoid using default communication protocols that may have known vulnerabilities.

3. **Intrusion Detection and Prevention Systems (IDPS):**
   - Deploy IDPS to monitor IoT networks for unusual activity and potential security threats.

- Utilize anomaly detection and machine learning techniques to identify and respond to previously unknown attack patterns.

4. Firmware and Software Security:
- Ensure that IoT devices run firmware and software that are regularly updated and patched.
- Use secure boot mechanisms to verify the integrity of firmware and software during device startup.

5. Physical Security:
- Protect IoT devices from physical tampering or unauthorized access, especially those deployed in public or remote locations.
- Implement tamper-evident seals and enclosures for critical devices.

IoT Security Standards and Frameworks:
Adhering to established IoT security standards and frameworks can help organizations implement best practices and ensure comprehensive security. Notable standards and frameworks include:

1. NIST Cybersecurity Framework:
Provides guidelines for managing and reducing

cybersecurity risks, including those related to IoT.

2. **IoT Cybersecurity Improvement Act:** A U.S. law that sets minimum security standards for IoT devices used by the federal government, which can serve as a benchmark for other organizations.

3. **ETSI EN 303 645:** A European standard that outlines security requirements for consumer IoT devices, focusing on areas such as data protection, software updates, and access control.

Emerging Trends and Future Directions in IoT Security:

As IoT continues to evolve, several emerging trends and future directions are shaping the landscape of IoT security:

1. **AI and Machine Learning:** Leveraging AI and machine learning for threat detection and response can enhance IoT security by identifying patterns and anomalies that may indicate cyber attacks.

2. **Blockchain Technology:** Using blockchain for secure, decentralized IoT networks can improve data integrity and trustworthiness by providing tamper-proof records of device interactions and transactions.

3. **Edge Computing:** Shifting data processing and analysis to the edge of the network, closer to IoT devices, can reduce latency and enhance security by minimizing the need to transmit sensitive data over the internet.

4. **Post-Quantum Cryptography:** Preparing for the future threat of quantum computing, which could potentially break current encryption methods, by developing and implementing post-quantum cryptographic algorithms.

Frequently Asked Questions And Answers

1. What are the primary security challenges in IoT?

   - The primary security challenges in IoT include device diversity and scale, resource constraints, long device lifespans with infrequent updates, and network complexity. These factors contribute to a vast and complex attack surface, making IoT devices vulnerable to various cyber threats.

2. What does 'secure by design' mean in the context of IoT?

   - 'Secure by design' means incorporating security measures during the design and development phase of IoT devices. This approach ensures that security features are built into the device from the outset, rather than being added later as an afterthought, making the devices inherently more secure.

3. How can data be protected in IoT environments?

   - Data in IoT environments can be protected by encrypting it both at rest and in transit, using strong encryption protocols. Implementing data loss prevention (DLP) solutions and regularly backing up data are also critical measures to prevent unauthorized access and ensure data integrity.

4. What is the importance of Identity and Access Management (IAM) in IoT?

- IAM is crucial in IoT because it controls who can access IoT devices and systems, and what actions they can perform. Strong authentication and authorization mechanisms, such as multi-factor authentication (MFA) and role-based access control (RBAC), help prevent unauthorized access and potential misuse of IoT devices and data.

5. Why is network segmentation important for IoT security?

- Network segmentation involves dividing a network into smaller segments or subnetworks, each with its own security controls. This limits the spread of an attack by containing it within a segment, protecting critical systems and sensitive data from being compromised if one part of the network is breached.

6. How can IoT devices be secured against physical tampering?

- IoT devices can be secured against physical tampering by using tamper-evident seals, secure enclosures, and physical access controls. Devices deployed in public or remote locations should be protected with robust physical security measures to prevent unauthorized access and tampering.

7. What role do Intrusion Detection and Prevention Systems (IDPS) play in IoT security?

- IDPS monitor IoT networks for unusual activity and potential security threats. They use techniques such as anomaly detection and machine learning to identify suspicious behavior and respond to potential attacks, enhancing the overall security of IoT environments.

8. What are the key compliance considerations for IoT security?

- Key compliance considerations for IoT security include adhering to data residency and sovereignty laws, meeting industry-specific regulatory requirements such as GDPR, HIPAA, and PCI DSS, and maintaining detailed logs and reports to demonstrate compliance and support audits.

9. How can businesses ensure regular updates and patch management for IoT devices?

- Businesses can ensure regular updates and patch management by implementing automated update mechanisms, establishing a process for timely distribution and application of security patches, and monitoring devices for compliance with update policies. Regular updates help protect devices from known vulnerabilities and emerging threats.

10. What emerging trends are shaping the future of IoT security?

- Emerging trends in IoT security include the use of artificial intelligence (AI) and machine learning for enhanced threat detection, blockchain technology for secure, decentralized networks, edge computing for localized data processing and security, and post-quantum cryptography to prepare for future quantum computing threats.

11. What steps should organizations take to respond to IoT security incidents?

- Organizations should have an incident response plan that includes steps for detecting, containing, eradicating, and recovering from security incidents. Regularly testing and updating the incident response plan ensures its effectiveness. Additionally, organizations should conduct post-incident analysis to learn from incidents and improve security measures.

12. How can blockchain technology enhance IoT security?

- Blockchain technology can enhance IoT security by providing a tamper-proof ledger for recording device interactions and transactions. This decentralized approach improves data integrity and trustworthiness, making it harder for attackers to alter records or gain unauthorized access to IoT systems.

Chapter 11: The Future of Cybersecurity

We delve into the future of cybersecurity, exploring emerging trends, technologies, and strategies that will shape the cybersecurity landscape in the coming years. As technology evolves and cyber threats become more sophisticated, understanding the future trajectory of cybersecurity is crucial for preparing and adapting to new challenges.

Emerging Threats and Challenges

1. **Advanced Persistent Threats (APTs):**

   - APTs are long-term, targeted attacks carried out by sophisticated adversaries, often nation-states or well-funded criminal organizations. These threats are characterized by their persistence and stealth, aiming to gain and maintain unauthorized access to networks and systems over extended periods.

   - Future APTs are expected to employ more advanced techniques, including leveraging AI to evade detection and exploiting vulnerabilities in emerging technologies like IoT and 5G networks.

2. **Ransomware Evolution:**

- Ransomware attacks have become increasingly prevalent and damaging. Future ransomware strains are likely to become more sophisticated, using advanced encryption methods, exfiltration tactics, and targeting critical infrastructure.

- The rise of Ransomware-as-a-Service (RaaS) platforms, where cybercriminals provide ransomware tools to less skilled attackers, will further proliferate ransomware threats.

3. Supply Chain Attacks:

- Cybercriminals target vulnerabilities in an organization's supply chain to compromise systems and data. These attacks can be particularly damaging because they exploit trusted relationships between businesses and their suppliers.

- As supply chains become more interconnected and complex, securing them will require enhanced visibility, stronger third-party risk management, and collaboration between organizations.

4. Quantum Computing Threats:

- Quantum computing has the potential to revolutionize many fields, including cybersecurity. However, it also poses a significant threat to current cryptographic algorithms, which could be rendered obsolete by quantum computers capable of breaking traditional encryption methods.

- Preparing for this future involves developing and adopting quantum-resistant cryptographic algorithms to ensure the security of sensitive data.

Emerging Technologies and Innovations

1. Artificial Intelligence (AI) and Machine Learning (ML):

- AI and ML are transforming cybersecurity by enhancing threat detection, response, and prediction capabilities. These technologies can analyze vast amounts of data to identify patterns and anomalies indicative of cyber threats.

- Future applications of AI and ML in cybersecurity include automated threat hunting, advanced behavioral analytics, and adaptive security measures that evolve with the threat landscape.

2. Zero Trust Architecture:

- The Zero Trust security model operates on the principle of "never trust, always verify," requiring continuous verification of user identities and access privileges regardless of their location within or outside the network.

 - Implementing Zero Trust involves micro-segmentation, robust identity and access management (IAM), and continuous monitoring. This approach helps mitigate the risks of insider threats and lateral movement within networks.

3. Blockchain and Decentralized Security:

 - Blockchain technology offers a decentralized approach to securing data and transactions, providing transparency, immutability, and tamper-proof records.

 - Future applications of blockchain in cybersecurity include secure identity management, supply chain security, and the protection of critical infrastructure. Decentralized security solutions can reduce single points of failure and enhance data integrity.

4. 5G and Beyond:

 - The deployment of 5G networks promises faster speeds, lower latency, and greater connectivity. However, it also introduces new security challenges, including increased attack surfaces and the potential for more sophisticated cyber attacks.

- Securing 5G networks will require robust encryption, network slicing, and collaboration between telecommunications providers, manufacturers, and regulatory bodies.

Strategies for Future Cybersecurity

1. Proactive Threat Intelligence:

- Proactive threat intelligence involves gathering and analyzing data on emerging threats, attack vectors, and adversary tactics to anticipate and mitigate potential cyber attacks.

- Organizations should invest in threat intelligence platforms, collaborate with industry peers, and participate in information-sharing initiatives to stay ahead of evolving threats.

2. Enhanced Incident Response and Recovery:

- Effective incident response and recovery plans are critical for minimizing the impact of cyber attacks. Future strategies will focus on automation, orchestration, and continuous improvement of response capabilities.

- Leveraging AI and ML for automated incident detection and response can significantly reduce response times and improve overall resilience.

3. **Security by Design and Privacy by Design:**

   - Integrating security and privacy principles into the design and development of systems, applications, and devices ensures that they are secure from the outset.

   - Adopting a holistic approach to security and privacy by design involves conducting thorough risk assessments, implementing robust security controls, and continuously monitoring for vulnerabilities.

4. **Human-Centric Security:**

   - Despite advances in technology, human factors remain a critical aspect of cybersecurity. Future strategies will focus on enhancing security awareness, training, and education for employees and stakeholders.

   - Developing a security-conscious culture, encouraging responsible behavior, and fostering collaboration between security teams and other departments are essential for reducing human-related security risks.

Preparing for the Future

1. Continuous Learning and Adaptation:

- The cybersecurity landscape is constantly evolving, requiring organizations to stay informed about emerging threats, technologies, and best practices. Continuous learning and adaptation are crucial for maintaining a robust security posture.

- Investing in professional development, attending industry conferences, and participating in cybersecurity forums can help security professionals stay current with the latest trends and innovations.

2. Regulatory Compliance and Governance:

- Regulatory requirements and standards will continue to evolve, reflecting new threats and technological advancements. Organizations must stay compliant with relevant regulations and implement strong governance frameworks to manage cybersecurity risks effectively.

- Regular audits, risk assessments, and adherence to industry standards such as GDPR, NIST, and ISO/IEC 27001 are essential for maintaining compliance and enhancing security.

3. **Collaboration and Public-Private Partnerships:**

- Collaboration between the public and private sectors is vital for addressing complex cybersecurity challenges. Public-private partnerships can facilitate information sharing, joint threat intelligence efforts, and coordinated responses to cyber incidents.

- Engaging with government agencies, industry associations, and cybersecurity alliances can enhance collective security efforts and contribute to a safer digital ecosystem.

Frequently Asked Questions And Answers

1. What are Advanced Persistent Threats (APTs) and why are they significant?

   - APTs are sophisticated, long-term targeted attacks often conducted by nation-states or well-funded criminal organizations. They aim to maintain unauthorized access to networks for extended periods. APTs are significant because they can cause extensive damage and steal sensitive information without detection for long periods.

2. How is ransomware expected to evolve in the future?

   - Ransomware is likely to become more sophisticated, employing advanced encryption and exfiltration techniques. The rise of Ransomware-as-a-Service (RaaS) will make it easier for less skilled attackers to launch ransomware attacks. Future strains may target critical infrastructure more frequently, causing widespread disruption.

3. What is the impact of quantum computing on cybersecurity?

   - Quantum computing has the potential to break current cryptographic algorithms, making traditional encryption methods obsolete. This poses a significant threat to data security. Preparing for this future involves developing and adopting quantum-resistant cryptographic algorithms to protect sensitive information.

4. How can AI and machine learning enhance cybersecurity?

- AI and machine learning can improve cybersecurity by enhancing threat detection, response, and prediction capabilities. They can analyze vast amounts of data to identify patterns and anomalies indicative of cyber threats, automate threat hunting, and provide adaptive security measures that evolve with the threat landscape.

5. What is Zero Trust Architecture and how does it improve security?

- Zero Trust Architecture operates on the principle of "never trust, always verify," requiring continuous verification of user identities and access privileges regardless of their location. It improves security by implementing micro-segmentation, robust identity and access management (IAM), and continuous monitoring, thereby reducing the risk of insider threats and lateral movement within networks.

6. How can blockchain technology be used to enhance cybersecurity?

- Blockchain technology offers a decentralized approach to securing data and transactions, providing transparency, immutability, and tamper-proof records. It can be used for secure identity management, supply chain security, and protecting critical infrastructure, reducing single points of failure and enhancing data integrity.

7. What are the security challenges associated with 5G networks?

- 5G networks introduce new security challenges due to increased attack surfaces and potential for more sophisticated cyber attacks. Securing 5G networks requires robust encryption, network slicing, and collaboration between telecommunications providers, manufacturers, and regulatory bodies to address these challenges effectively.

8. What is the role of proactive threat intelligence in future cybersecurity?

- Proactive threat intelligence involves gathering and analyzing data on emerging threats, attack vectors, and adversary tactics to anticipate and mitigate potential cyber attacks. It enables organizations to stay ahead of evolving threats, invest in threat intelligence platforms, and participate in information-sharing initiatives for improved security.

9. How can organizations enhance their incident response and recovery capabilities?
   - Organizations can enhance their incident response and recovery capabilities by implementing automated detection and response mechanisms, orchestrating response efforts, and continuously improving their incident response plans. Leveraging AI and ML for automated incident detection and response can significantly reduce response times and improve overall resilience.

10. What does 'security by design' and 'privacy by design' mean?
   - 'Security by design' and 'privacy by design' refer to integrating security and privacy principles into the design and development of systems, applications, and devices from the outset. This approach ensures that security and privacy are considered at every stage, reducing

vulnerabilities and enhancing overall security and data protection.

11. Why is a human-centric approach important in cybersecurity?

- A human-centric approach is important because human factors remain a critical aspect of cybersecurity. Enhancing security awareness, training, and education for employees and stakeholders, developing a security-conscious culture, and encouraging responsible behavior are essential for reducing human-related security risks.

12. How can organizations prepare for future cybersecurity challenges?

- Organizations can prepare for future cybersecurity challenges by staying informed about emerging threats and technologies, investing in advanced security technologies, fostering a security-conscious culture, adhering to regulatory requirements, and collaborating with industry peers and public-private partnerships. Continuous learning, adaptation, and proactive strategies are crucial for maintaining a robust security posture.

Conclusion

The future of cybersecurity will be shaped by emerging threats, innovative technologies, and evolving strategies. As the digital landscape becomes more complex and interconnected, the need for robust, adaptive, and proactive cybersecurity measures will only intensify. Organizations must embrace a comprehensive approach to cybersecurity that encompasses technology, processes, and people to protect their assets, data, and operations in an increasingly digital world.

By staying informed about future trends, investing in advanced security technologies, and fostering a security-conscious culture, organizations can navigate the challenges and opportunities of the future cybersecurity landscape. Ultimately, a proactive and resilient cybersecurity strategy will be essential for safeguarding the digital future and ensuring the continued growth and innovation of businesses and societies.

www.ingramcontent.com/pod-product-compliance
Lightning Source LLC
Chambersburg PA
CBHW071259050326
40690CB00011B/2455